DATE DUE		
MR 3 '92		11/28/01 CSH R
AP 25 '92	MY 16'97	DEC 2 9 2001
DE 11 '92	JUN 10, '97	
AP 1 '93		
SE 7 '93		
FEB 23 '94		
MR 16 '95		
FE 21 '95		
MR 28 '95		
261-2500		Printed in USA

ON THEIR TOES,
A RUSSIAN BALLET SCHOOL.

BY ANN MORRIS
PHOTOGRAPHS BY KEN HEYMAN

ATHENEUM 1991 NEW YORK

MAXWELL MACMILLAN CANADA
Toronto

MAXWELL MACMILLAN INTERNATIONAL
New York Oxford Singapore Sydney

Atheneum
Macmillan Publishing Company
866 Third Avenue
New York, NY 10022

Maxwell Macmillan Canada, Inc.
1200 Eglinton Avenue East
Suite 200
Don Mills, Ontario M3C 3N1

Macmillan Publishing Company is part of the
Maxwell Communication Group of Companies.

First edition
Printed in the United States of America
10 9 8 7 6 5 4 3 2 1
The text of this book is set in Cheltenham Light

Library of Congress Cataloging-in-Publication Data
Morris, Ann, 1930–
On their toes: a Russian ballet school / Ann Morris; photographs
by Ken Heyman. — 1st ed.
p.   cm.
Summary: A behind-the-scenes look at the Vaganova Choreographic Institute,
a training school for young dancers in the Soviet Union.
ISBN 0-689-31660-7
1. Leningradskoe akademicheskoe khoreograficheskoe uchilishche im.
A. IA. Vaganovoy—Juvenile literature. 2. Ballet—Study and
teaching—Russian S.F.S.R.—Leningrad—Case studies—Juvenile
literature. [1. Kirov Ballet Academy. 2. Ballet dancing.]
I. Heyman, Ken, ill. II. Title.
GV1788.6.L466M67   1991
792.8'0947'453—dc20   91–11903

SPACIBO MEANS THANK YOU!

When you go to the Soviet Union you must make many plans in advance and get very good advice. I would like to thank all the people who gave such advice and assistance in the planning and production of this book.

In the office of the Russian Consulate in Washington, Vladimir Zaretsky first put me in touch with Novosti Press in Moscow, which would pave the way for my first research visit and hasten the arrival of my precious visa, which finally appeared on the morning of my departure.

Margo, Natasha, and Marsha at Margo Tours in New York were consistently reassuring, informative, and ultimately practical about travel and living arrangements.

Sergei Morozov from Novosti met me at the airport with an armful of roses, as is the Russian custom, and was a most sympathetic guide.

Leonid Nikolayezich Nadirov, the director of the Vaganova Choreographic Institute, understood the needs of a writer and photographer. It was he who made all the arrangements at the school so that Ken Heyman and I could do our job. Marina Vivien at the school's museum was a valuable source of information about the school's traditions. The children's special teacher and friend, Ira Terentyeva, was both hostess and helper in getting Ken and me to the right place at the right time. We felt that she became a friend to us as well.

My endless gratitude to Alla Grikurova, our translator on whom we depended to "talk" with the children and teachers. It was Alla who took me to my first performance at the Kirov Ballet Theater. And it was Alla who, with her wonderful sense of humor and perfect American slang, became our most articulate voice. Thanks also to her husband, Sergei, who drove us patiently around the city and endured our never-ending work schedule.

In London the ballet writer Margaret Willis was generous with her enthusiasm for the project and with introductions to her ballet friends in Leningrad.

Elizabeth Kendall, the dance critic, whom I met at the breakfast table in Leningrad, proved to be a most helpful consultant and supportive friend. Her special interest in the Kirov and extensive knowledge of the history of dance added considerably to the richness of our stay in the Soviet Union and to my own understanding of Russian ballet.

The famous teacher Ninel Kurgapkina was kind enough to look at the photos with me in New York as we were preparing the book, as was the former Vaganova Academy pupil Elena Kunikova. Both of them made useful suggestions.

Finally, and most of all, we would like to say *spacibo* to the children and their families and teachers of "Theater Street," who were the inspiration for this book. Our hope is that in some way this story about them will provide American children with a feeling and understanding about their art and their lives in this beautiful and historic city of Leningrad.

If you walk down Rossi Street in Leningrad, you might see boys and girls with their arms linked laughing and talking about their favorite dancer or what they will wear in a performance that evening. This beautiful street, often called "Theater Street," is the home of the Vaganova Choreographic Institute, which prepares dancers for the Kirov Ballet.

And these are the children of one of the world's most famous ballet schools. Most people call it the Kirov Ballet Academy, although it trains young dancers for ballet theaters throughout the Soviet Union and in many other parts of the world. Over one thousand children from all over the Soviet Union apply each year, but only about seventy are selected, and it is a great honor to be chosen.

In the school museum are pictures of the famous dancers: Anna Pavlova, Vaslav Nijinsky, and George Ballanchine; and more recently Natalia Makarova, Rudolph Nureyev, and Mikhail Baryshnikov. All have attended classes there and have become world figures on the ballet stage. Many of the students will become famous dancers too, but it will take many years of practice and patience. They will have less time for play than most children, but for them dancing is their play. They prefer dancing to anything else in the world.

Each day the children begin their classes at the barre, where they do special exercises to strengthen their muscles and warm their bodies. The exercises also lessen the possibility of injury. If the students miss more than a day of exercise, their bodies will not do all the things they want them to do. There's a Russian saying: "If you don't take class for two days, you notice. If you don't take class for four days, everyone notices."

The color of the students' dance clothes identifies the class that they are in. At the Kirov Academy the ten-year-olds in the first class always wear white. From the second class on, the girls dress in black leotards and the boys in white shirts and black tights.

Ballet in the Soviet Union is rich with tradition. The children who go to this school know that they follow in the tradition of imperial Russia, before the Revolution, when the czar built what was then called the Maryinsky Theater.

Under a picture of the famous dancer Anna Pavlova these more experienced dancers take class with their teacher, Galina Novitskaya, who was once a dancer too. She watches them and shows them how to hold their shoulders, arms, and bodies in the correct position.

Kirov dancers are taught that the upper part of their bodies is the most expressive. They move more slowly than dancers in the West, though perhaps with greater elegance. You might say that the harmony and classical beauty of Leningrad has served to influence their art. In the West, dancers trained by teachers influenced by George Ballanchine move faster. Their legs are considered as expressive as the upper half of the body. This speed might well be a reflection of the fast and energetic pace of life in New York.

About one-third of the students in the school are boys. They have the same academic classes as the girls and additional classes in fencing and gymnastics. Boys need to develop a special kind of strength so they will be able to lift their partners. Their teacher, Vasily Ivanov, was formerly a dancer at the Kirov Ballet.

The brown spots on the floor are from the water that is sprinkled on it to help prevent slipping. The sloping wooden floor of the rehearsal room is similar to the floor at the Kirov Ballet Theater. The Russians design their ballet stages that way so that the audience can more easily see the feet of the dancers.

Sore feet and bruised legs are part of a dancer's life. Sasha gets physical therapy in the infirmary where the children go with all their illnesses and injuries. Keeping healthy is certainly important for these young dancers. They must eat well and get plenty of sleep in order to have the energy to dance for so many hours and to keep up with their studies as well.

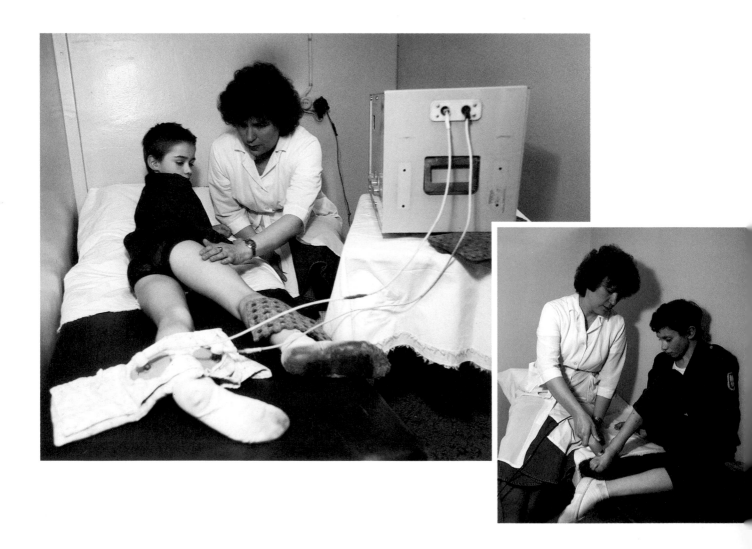

The children take their academic classes in the same building as their dance classes. In addition to their daily dance class, which is called "classics," they study mathematics, geography, history, physics, chemistry, zoology, biology, literature, and Russian. Every student also learns French, which is the language of ballet. Parents must sign a record book every Saturday which shows their child's progress in each of their subjects. Reports on classics are given quarterly. Children are rated on professional technique, attitude, and how well they perform.

Maya catches a moment in geography class to talk with her friends. The ballet-school children enjoy their share of fun and mischief, but good manners are always stressed. The children rise from their desks when anyone enters the room. When responding to a question they raise their hand with the small finger forward, and stand up when their teacher calls on them. As a mark of respect to adults the girls curtsy and the boys bow their heads ever so slightly when passing them in the hall.

Music is also a very important part of the curriculum. The students must understand what each of the composers is trying to convey in the ballet. There are classes in the history of dance, painting, mime, folk dancing, and acting. Between classes, groups of children can be found watching videotapes of such famous dancers as Fred Astaire, Shirley Temple, and Bill Robinson. Tapes of Petroushka, and of Isadora Duncan's trip to the Soviet Union, are also useful for their study of the history of dance.

Though these children work very hard, there's always time for ice cream along Leningrad's main street, Nevsky Prospekt.

Street artists draw Maya's and Kolya's portraits.

The dancers play in a park in one of the many
historic parts of the city.

At home Sveta shows her parents, who are also dancers, some of the steps she has learned this week. "Even when she's tired, Sveta dances in the apartment," says her mother. "She was always like that. When she was a tiny baby we took her to the theater when we couldn't get a baby-sitter. She always wanted to dance."

Sveta strokes her cat, Buran, which means *storm* in Russian.

Sveta's mother was a dancer at the Maly Theater, the second most important ballet theater in Leningrad. Her scrapbook is filled with pictures of her in her many roles. Sveta's father is now a representative of the union for ballet dancers. He is very proud of Sveta and likes to tell about her very first part, as a boy in the opera *Madame Butterfly* when she was four.

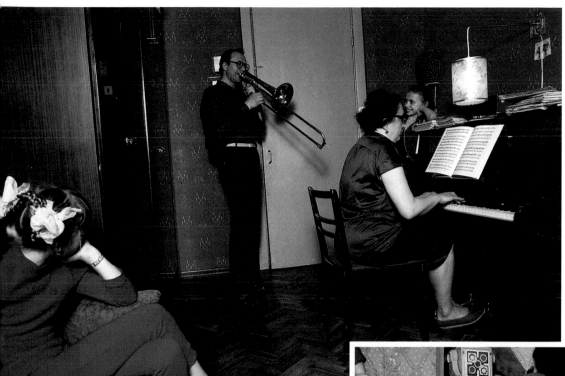

At Maya's home it is time for tea, which is often the case in the Soviet Union. Maya's mother pours for her and her sister Vica, who is a gymnast.

Both their parents are musicians, so music has been a part of Maya's life since she was very small. This will help her in her dancing. Their father's other hobby is sewing clothes for his children.

The children who do not live in Leningrad live together in a dormitory, which is like a big home. Pictures of famous dancers and teachers line the walls. Stuffed animals and pictures of family keep the children from getting homesick. The older children become "mothers" to the younger ones. All of them must spend time each day washing their dance clothes and helping with chores around the dormitory. These children spend their winter holidays in the country, where they ski and skate. In the summer they go to the Black Sea. Although they spend little time with their own parents, these students are often invited to the homes of the children who live in Leningrad.

Each month there is a birthday party for any or all of the children whose birthdays came that month. This month the party is for Aliya Sapugova, whose home is far away in Alma-Ata, Kazakhstan.

Ira Terentyeva is their teacher and friend. She helps them with their schedules and activities and is always there to share all their excitement as well as their problems. In recent years the school has been guided by a council consisting of both teachers and some of the senior students.

Maya, Sveta, and Ira meet in front of the famous Kirov Ballet Theater before attending a performance of *Giselle*. Children have many roles in the Kirov ballet as fairies, pages, mice, even princes and princesses. When they are performing in the ballet, they have long hours of rehearsals in addition to their usual classes.

Before a performance for their parents and teachers, Ira checks to see if the girls have sewn on their straps and mended their shoes properly. Each dancer uses about fifteen pairs of ballet shoes a year. Every time they dance in a production of the Kirov they are given a new pair of shoes. It is the tradition for girls to wear pink shoes and boys to wear white. As the boys do not dance on their toes, they always wear soft shoes.

The locker room is a
good place for the dancers
to catch up on the latest
news while they repair their
shoes. There's always
excitement when the
children discover an article
about themselves in a new
magazine.

It takes these dancers several hours to put on their makeup and do their hair before a performance. Special classes in makeup are part of the curriculum.

Finally the performers are
fitted into their costumes.

Backstage, the dancers warm up. Some of the dancers wear leg warmers to keep their muscles relaxed and agile.

Curtain up! The young dancers perform excerpts from several different ballets: *Sleeping Beauty, Swan Lake, Chopiniana* (called *Les Sylphides* in the West). Their parents and teachers are all very excited and very pleased.

Bravo! The dancers take a bow. When the audience
applauds all the hard work is rewarded.